AIRBNB UNLOCKED

Start and Scale your Rental Arbitrage Business

By Supercrown Vault

TABLE OF CONTENTS

Introduction

Unlocking the Doors to Airbnb and VRBO Rental Arbitrage Success

In the ever-evolving landscape of the gig economy, an intriguing opportunity has emerged for entrepreneurs and investors alike: Airbnb and VRBO rental arbitrage. This innovative business model, which involves renting a property to subsequently re-rent it on short-term rental platforms, has opened up a new avenue for generating income in the hospitality industry.

As we embark on this journey together through the pages of this book, we will delve into the intricacies of building a successful Airbnb and VRBO rental arbitrage business. From scouting the perfect location to mastering the art of guest satisfaction, this guide is designed to equip you with the knowledge and strategies needed to thrive in this competitive space.

The concept of rental arbitrage is simple yet powerful. By leveraging properties that you lease, rather than own, you can tap into the lucrative world of short-term rentals without the substantial capital typically required to purchase real estate. This model not only democratizes access to the hospitality industry but also introduces a layer of flexibility and scalability previously unattainable for individual entrepreneurs.

However, like any business venture, rental arbitrage comes with its challenges. Market saturation, regulatory hurdles, and operational complexities are just a few of the obstacles you might encounter. This book aims to navigate you through these potential pitfalls, providing practical advice and proven strategies to overcome them. You will learn how to conduct thorough market research, negotiate favorable lease terms, create compelling listings, and deliver exceptional guest experiences that drive repeat business.

Moreover, this book will delve into the nuances of managing your properties remotely, optimizing your pricing strategy, and utilizing technology to streamline your operations. Whether you are a seasoned real estate investor looking to diversify your portfolio or a newcomer seeking to make your mark in the short-term rental market, you will find valuable insights and actionable tips to help you succeed.

As we progress, remember that the essence of Airbnb and VRBO rental arbitrage lies in the experience you provide to your guests. In a world where personal touches and unique experiences stand out, your ability to create a memorable stay will set you apart from the competition. This book will guide you in curating spaces that not only meet the needs of your guests but also exceed their expectations, turning first-time visitors into loyal customers.

Welcome to the world of Airbnb and VRBO rental arbitrage. Your journey to building a thriving business in the short-term rental market begins here. Let's unlock the doors to success together.

Chapter 1

The Basics

Understanding Rental Arbitrage

Rental Arbitrage (RA) is a business model that operates on a relatively simple premise: you lease a property long-term and then rent it out on a short-term basis through platforms like Airbnb and VRBO. Unlike traditional property investment strategies, RA doesn't require you to own the properties, significantly lowering the barrier to entry for those looking to invest in the lucrative short-term rental market.

How Does It Work?

Imagine you find a charming apartment in a bustling city center. You sign a year-long lease with the landlord, with monthly rent set at $2,000. You then furnish and list the apartment on Airbnb and VRBO for $150 per night. If you manage to book the apartment for just 15 nights a month, you're looking at a gross income of $2,250 — a tidy profit after paying the rent, before considering other expenses such as utilities, cleaning, and platform fees.

The Appeal

The appeal of RA lies in its potential for high returns on investment. With careful management, the right location, and optimal pricing, you can achieve significantly higher income compared to traditional long-term rentals. Moreover, RA offers flexibility; you can scale up by leasing more properties or exit the business by not renewing leases, without the commitment and financial burden of owning real estate.

Navigating Short-term Rental Regulations

Entering the RA business requires a thorough understanding of the legal landscape surrounding short-term rentals, which can vary widely by location. Cities around the world have implemented a range of regulations, from complete bans to requiring special licenses or imposing taxes.

Why Regulations Matter

Regulations are often introduced to address concerns about housing shortages, neighborhood disruptions, and safety standards. Ignoring these laws can result in hefty fines, legal action, and being banned from hosting platforms. Therefore, understanding and complying with local regulations is critical for operating a successful RA business.

Examples of Regulatory Environments

- New York City: Strictly regulates short-term rentals, generally prohibiting rentals of entire apartments for less than 30 days unless the host is present.

- Austin, Texas: Requires short-term rental operators to obtain a license, imposes occupancy limits, and enforces specific noise ordinances.

These examples highlight the importance of conducting thorough research and possibly consulting legal experts to ensure compliance.

The Giants of Short-Term Rentals: Airbnb and VRBO

Airbnb and VRBO are two of the most prominent platforms in the short-term rental market, each with its unique characteristics and user base.

Airbnb

Founded in 2008, Airbnb has grown into a global community of millions of hosts and travelers. Its platform is renowned for offering a wide range of accommodations, from shared rooms to luxurious villas. Airbnb's success lies in its user-friendly interface, extensive review system, and commitment to creating a sense of belonging among its community.

VRBO

VRBO, which stands for Vacation Rentals by Owner, has been connecting property owners with travelers since 1995. Focused exclusively on whole-property rentals, VRBO is favored by families and larger groups seeking entire homes or condos for their vacations. Its straightforward listing and booking process appeals to both property owners and guests.

Market Impact

Together, Airbnb and VRBO have transformed the travel and hospitality industry, making short-term rentals a popular alternative to traditional hotels. For RA entrepreneurs, these platforms provide a ready-made marketplace to reach millions of potential guests.

Understanding the dynamics, fee structures, and guest expectations on each platform is essential for maximizing your success in rental arbitrage.

As we delve deeper into the world of rental arbitrage, it's clear that success hinges on a thorough understanding of the basics: recognizing the potential of RA as a business model, navigating the complex landscape of short-term rental regulations, and leveraging the power of platforms like Airbnb and VRBO. With this foundation, you're well on your way to building a profitable rental arbitrage business.

Chapter 2

Finding Profitable Markets & Properties

To build a successful Airbnb and VRBO Rental Arbitrage (RA) business, identifying the right markets and properties is crucial. This chapter dives into strategies and tools like AirDNA, Zillow, Airbnb neighborhood research, and Wheelhouse to help you pinpoint profitable opportunities.

Leveraging AirDNA for Market Analysis

AirDNA is a powerful analytics platform that provides data and insights on the performance of vacation rental properties across Airbnb and VRBO. It's an invaluable resource for RA entrepreneurs seeking to identify high-demand locations and understand market dynamics.

How to Use AirDNA

1. Market Minder: This feature offers a deep dive into specific markets, showing average daily rates, occupancy rates, seasonal trends, and revenue potentials. For example, if you're considering Austin, Texas, AirDNA can reveal which neighborhoods have the highest demand and the potential revenue you could expect.

2. Investment Explorer: Tailored for those scouting new investment opportunities, it ranks cities based on their investment potential, factoring in regulatory environments and financial performance of rentals.

Using AirDNA, you can assess which markets have the best balance of high demand, reasonable property costs, and friendly regulations, guiding your property selection process.

Finding Properties with Zillow.com

Zillow is a popular online real estate marketplace that can be used to find potential rental properties for your RA business. It offers comprehensive listings, including rental prices, which helps in identifying properties within your budget that can be profitable for short-term rentals.

Strategies for Using Zillow

- Search Filters: Use filters to narrow down properties based on your criteria such as location, price, number of bedrooms, and amenities. This can help you quickly identify properties that meet the demands of short-term renters.

- Market Comparison: Compare the rental prices listed on Zillow with the potential nightly rates you've identified through AirDNA. This will help you gauge the profitability of leasing a property for RA.

Airbnb Neighborhood Research

Understanding the nuances of different neighborhoods is critical in choosing the right property. Airbnb's own platform can be a treasure trove of information.

Conducting Research

- Browse Listings: Look at existing Airbnb listings in your target neighborhoods. Note the range of nightly rates, the style and quality of top-performing listings, and any amenities or features that are frequently highlighted.

- Read Reviews: Guest reviews can offer insights into what travelers value in a specific area, such as proximity to attractions, safety, and ease of transportation.

This hands-on approach gives you a clearer picture of what makes a property successful in a particular neighborhood.

Hypothetical Listing Research with Wheelhouse

Wheelhouse is a dynamic pricing tool that can also be used for market research. By creating a hypothetical listing, you can experiment with different pricing strategies and forecast your potential earnings.

How to Conduct Research with Wheelhouse

1. Create a Hypothetical Listing: Input details about your potential property, including location, size, and amenities.

2. Analyze Pricing Recommendations: Wheelhouse will provide pricing recommendations based on extensive market data. This helps you understand how much you could charge per night and anticipate monthly revenues.

By analyzing this data, you can make informed decisions about where to establish your RA business and which properties offer the best potential for profitability.

The journey to finding profitable markets and properties for your Airbnb and VRBO RA business requires diligent research and the effective use of tools like AirDNA, Zillow, Airbnb, and Wheelhouse.

By understanding market demands, analyzing potential earnings, and selecting the right properties, you can set the foundation for a successful RA venture. Remember, the key is not just finding a good property, but finding the right property in the right market at the right time.

Chapter 3

Pitching Landlords

Securing a property for Airbnb and VRBO rental arbitrage involves convincing landlords to entrust you with their property under a business model they might not be familiar with. This chapter will guide you through the process of pitching to landlords and negotiating a rental agreement that aligns with your business goals.

Understanding Landlords' Concerns

Before approaching landlords, it's essential to understand their potential concerns. Landlords might be wary about short-term rentals due to fears of property damage, legal issues, or the stability of rental income.

Your pitch should address these concerns directly, demonstrating how rental arbitrage can be beneficial for them.

Crafting Your Pitch

Your pitch to landlords should be professional, persuasive, and tailored to address their specific needs and concerns. Here's how to structure it:

Introduction: Present Yourself and Your Business

Begin by introducing yourself and your business. Explain your experience in the rental arbitrage market and highlight your professional approach to property management.

Benefits to the Landlord

- **Steady Income:** Emphasize that you will be leasing their property long-term, providing them with a consistent and reliable income.

- **Professional Property Management:** Assure them that the property will be professionally managed and maintained to a high standard, potentially reducing their maintenance costs over time.

- **Legal Compliance:** Highlight your commitment to complying with all local short-term rental regulations, mitigating the landlord's legal risks.

Addressing Concerns

- **Security Measures:** Explain the steps you will take to ensure the property is safe and secure, including vetting guests and installing security systems if necessary.

- **Insurance:** Discuss the insurance policies you will have in place to cover potential damages, offering peace of mind to the landlord.

The Proposal

Present your proposal, including the rent you're willing to pay, the lease term, and any other conditions. Be clear about your intentions to use the property for short-term rentals and how you plan to manage it.

Negotiating the Rental Agreement

Once a landlord shows interest, the next step is to negotiate a rental agreement that suits both parties. This agreement should be more detailed than a standard lease, addressing the specifics of your rental arbitrage business.

Key Components of the Agreement

- **Lease Term:** Agree on a lease term that gives you enough time to establish your business, typically at least one year.

- **Rent and Payment Terms:** Specify the rent amount, payment schedule, and any security deposit required.

- **Use of Property:** Clearly state that you will be using the property for short-term rentals. Include any restrictions or conditions the landlord requires.

- **Maintenance and Repairs:** Outline responsibilities for maintenance and repairs, ensuring the property remains in good condition.

- Subletting Clause: Ensure the agreement explicitly allows for subletting the property on short-term rental platforms.

Example of a Successful Pitch

Imagine you've found a desirable property in a popular tourist area. You approach the landlord with a well-prepared pitch, highlighting the benefits of consistent rental income, professional property management, and legal compliance.

You address their concerns by explaining your guest vetting process and showcasing your comprehensive insurance coverage. Finally, you present a fair proposal for a two-year lease, offering a slightly above-market rent to make the deal more attractive.

The landlord is impressed by your professionalism and the potential benefits of your proposal. After some negotiation, you agree on a rental rate, lease term, and conditions that are favorable to both parties. The agreement includes a clause that explicitly allows for short-term rentals, providing the legal foundation for your rental arbitrage business.

Pitching to landlords is a critical step in establishing a rental arbitrage business. By effectively communicating the benefits, addressing potential concerns, and negotiating a detailed rental agreement, you can secure the properties needed to launch and expand your venture. Remember, every successful pitch strengthens your position in the market and paves the way for future opportunities.

Chapter 4

Setting Up Your Property

Once you've successfully pitched to landlords and secured a property, the next crucial step is setting up and furnishing the property for Airbnb and VRBO. This chapter will guide you through optimizing your property setup, creating compelling listings, and maintaining high visibility in search engine results pages (SERP).

Setting Up and Furnishing a Property

The goal is to create a space that not only attracts guests but also encourages them to leave positive reviews, fostering higher occupancy rates.

Understanding Your Audience

Before purchasing furniture and decor, consider the target audience for your property. Are you catering to business travelers, families, or tourists seeking local experiences? Your furnishings and amenities should reflect the needs and preferences of your intended guests.

Essential Furnishings and Decor

- Functional and Comfortable Furniture: Invest in quality beds, sofas, and dining furniture to ensure guest comfort.

- A Well-Equipped Kitchen: Include all necessary appliances, cookware, and utensils.

- High-Quality Linens: Provide plush towels and high-thread-count sheets.

- Decor and Personal Touches: Add artwork and decor that reflect the local culture or create a welcoming atmosphere.

Smart Investments

- Durable Materials: Choose materials that are durable and easy to clean, reducing maintenance and replacement costs.

- Smart Home Devices: Install smart locks for easy check-in and check-out, and consider a smart thermostat to manage energy costs.

New Property Setup for Airbnb

Once your property is furnished, it's time to create your Airbnb listing.

Listing Details

- Title and Description: Craft a compelling title and detailed description that highlights the unique features of your property and the experiences guests can enjoy in the area.

- Amenities: Clearly list all amenities, including Wi-Fi, parking, and any extras like coffee machines or a hot tub.

- House Rules: Set clear house rules regarding noise, pets, and smoking to ensure guests know what is expected.

Other Elements of New Listings

- Guidebook: Create a digital guidebook for your guests that includes instructions for appliances, local recommendations, and emergency contact information.

- Pricing Strategy: Use dynamic pricing tools like Wheelhouse or Airbnb's pricing suggestions to set competitive rates that adjust for seasonality and local events.

Maintaining High SERP Rankings

Your property's visibility on Airbnb and VRBO is crucial. High SERP rankings lead to more views and bookings.

Tips for High Rankings

- Optimize Your Listing: Use keywords in your title and description that potential guests might search for.

- Update Regularly: Regularly update your listing with any new amenities or improvements.

- Encourage Reviews: Promptly ask guests to leave a review after their stay, as listings with more reviews tend to rank higher.

- Responsive Hosting: Respond quickly to inquiries and maintain a high response rate.

Photography for Airbnb Listing

Professional-quality photos are essential for making your listing stand out.

Photography Tips

- Hire a Professional: If possible, hire a professional photographer who has experience with real estate or hospitality photography.
- Showcase Key Areas: Ensure your photos highlight the best features of your property, including the living area, bedrooms, and any unique amenities.
- Use Natural Light: Take photos during the day when natural light is abundant to make spaces appear brighter and more welcoming.
- Include Local Attractions: Add a few photos of nearby attractions or scenic spots to entice guests interested in exploring the area.

Setting up and listing your property requires attention to detail, from furnishing and decor to optimizing your Airbnb and VRBO listings. By creating a welcoming, well-equipped space and employing strategies to maintain high SERP rankings, you can increase your property's visibility and appeal, leading to higher occupancy rates and a successful rental arbitrage business.

Remember, your property's presentation and the experience you offer will set you apart in the competitive short-term rental market.

Chapter 5

Behind the Scenes

Running a successful Airbnb and VRBO Rental Arbitrage business involves much more than just securing properties and setting them up for guests. This chapter dives into the essential behind-the-scenes operations, from customer service excellence and automation to legal considerations and scaling your business.

Handling Customer Service

Exceptional customer service is the cornerstone of a thriving rental arbitrage business. It not only ensures guest satisfaction but also significantly impacts your ratings and ability to become a superhost.

Tips for Stellar Customer Service

- Prompt Communication: Always respond to inquiries and concerns quickly and professionally.
- Personalized Experiences: Consider leaving personalized notes or welcome gifts for guests.
- Resolve Issues Swiftly: Address any problems immediately to minimize inconvenience to your guests.

Becoming a Superhost

Airbnb's Superhost program rewards hosts who go above and beyond in providing exceptional guest experiences. Achieving Superhost status can increase your visibility and attractiveness to potential guests.

Requirements and Benefits

- High Response Rate: Maintain a 90% or higher response rate.
- Positive Reviews: Achieve a high overall rating from guests.
- Minimum Bookings: Fulfill a minimum number of stays or nights per year.
- Low Cancellation Rate: Avoid canceling on guests, with exceptions for emergencies.

Becoming a Superhost enhances your listing's SERP ranking and instills trust in potential guests.

Automating Efforts

Efficiency is key to scaling your rental arbitrage business. Automation tools can save time and reduce the workload of managing multiple properties.

Automation Strategies

- Automated Messaging: Use tools to send pre-arrival instructions, welcome messages, and check-out reminders automatically.
- Smart Locks: Implement smart locks for keyless entry, allowing for seamless check-in and check-out without needing to be present.

- Dynamic Pricing Tools: Employ pricing software to automatically adjust your nightly rates based on market demand.

Getting a Short-Term Rental (STR) Permit

Many municipalities require STR permits to legally operate. Obtaining a permit ensures compliance with local regulations and avoids potential fines.

Steps to Acquire a STR Permit

1. Research Local Regulations: Understand the requirements and restrictions in your area.
2. Prepare Your Application: Gather necessary documents, such as proof of insurance and property ownership or lease agreement.
3. Compliance Inspection: Some locales may require a safety inspection of the property.
4. Submit Application and Fees: Complete the application process and pay any required fees.

Scaling Your Business

Scaling involves expanding your portfolio of properties to increase revenue. However, it requires careful planning and management to ensure profitability.

Considerations for Scaling

- Market Diversification: Explore new markets to reduce dependency on a single location.
- Operational Efficiency: Streamline operations to manage additional properties without compromising quality.
- Financial Management: Monitor cash flow and secure financing for expansion responsibly.

Setting Expectations and Incorporating Your Business

Treating your rental arbitrage venture as a professional business is crucial for long-term success.

Benefits of Incorporation

- Limited Liability: Protect your personal assets from business-related lawsuits.
- Tax Advantages: Potential tax benefits and deductions specific to businesses.
- Professional Image: Enhances credibility with landlords, guests, and financial institutions.

Preventing Costly Mistakes

Mistakes in the STR business can be expensive, from legal issues to property damage.

Strategies to Avoid Pitfalls

- Regular Maintenance: Prevent costly repairs with routine property inspections and maintenance.
- Insurance: Ensure you have comprehensive insurance coverage tailored for short-term rentals.
- Legal Compliance: Stay informed about local STR regulations and tax obligations.

Handling AirCover Claims

Airbnb's AirCover provides protection against damages and liability. Understanding how to navigate claims can help recover costs in the event of guest-caused damage.

Tips for Successful Claims

- Documentation: Keep detailed records and photographs of your property before and after each stay.
- Timely Reporting: Report any damages to Airbnb promptly, following their procedure for claims.

The behind-the-scenes management of an Airbnb and VRBO Rental Arbitrage business involves a mix of excellent customer service, operational efficiency, legal compliance, and strategic scaling. By focusing on these critical aspects, you can build a robust, profitable, and sustainable business that stands out in the competitive short-term rental market.

Remember, success in this industry comes from not just what your guests see, but also the unseen efforts that ensure their stay is memorable for all the right reasons.

Chapter 6

Property Cleaning & Management

Efficient property cleaning and management are pivotal to maintaining high-quality listings and ensuring guest satisfaction in your Airbnb and VRBO rental arbitrage business. This chapter explores strategies for sourcing reliable cleaners, establishing an effective property management system, and utilizing platforms like TurnoverBnB to streamline operations.

Finding and Sourcing Cleaners

The cleanliness of your properties directly impacts guest experiences and reviews, which in turn affect your bookings and revenue. Finding dependable and skilled cleaning services is therefore essential.

Tips for Sourcing Cleaners

- Local Networks: Tap into local real estate or short-term rental groups and forums to ask for recommendations.

- Online Platforms: Use websites like Craigslist, Thumbtack, or even LinkedIn to find cleaning services specializing in short-term rentals.

- Interview Process: Conduct interviews to assess their experience, reliability, and understanding of Airbnb and VRBO cleaning standards.

Building a Relationship

- Clear Expectations: Communicate your expectations regarding the level of cleanliness, turnaround times, and any specific tasks required, such as restocking supplies.

- Regular Feedback: Provide regular feedback to ensure quality is maintained and address any issues promptly.

Setting Up a Property Management System

A robust property management system is crucial for coordinating bookings, cleaning schedules, maintenance tasks, and communication with guests across multiple properties.

Components of an Effective System

- Digital Calendar: Use a digital calendar to track bookings from different platforms, scheduled cleanings, and maintenance appointments.

- Task Lists and Reminders: Implement a system for creating task lists for cleaners and maintenance teams, with automated reminders for upcoming tasks.

- Guest Communication: Set up automated messages for guest inquiries, booking confirmations, check-in instructions, and check-out reminders.

Software Solutions

Consider property management software designed for short-term rentals, such as Guesty or Tokeet, which offer integrated tools for managing bookings, payments, communication, and staff tasks.

Using TurnoverBnB

TurnoverBnB is a platform specifically designed to connect vacation rental hosts with local cleaners. It also provides tools to schedule cleanings automatically based on your Airbnb and VRBO calendar, ensuring your properties are always guest-ready.

How to Utilize TurnoverBnB

- Integration: Connect your TurnoverBnB account with your Airbnb and VRBO listings to sync booking calendars.

- Finding Cleaners: Use the platform to find and hire cleaners with experience in short-term rental turnovers. You can view ratings and reviews from other hosts.

- Scheduling and Payments: Schedule cleanings automatically following guest check-outs. The platform also facilitates direct payments to cleaners, simplifying the process.

Benefits of TurnoverBnB

- Efficiency: Automating the scheduling of cleanings reduces the risk of human error and ensures your properties are always prepared for new guests.

- Quality Control: Access to reviews and ratings helps in selecting reliable cleaners, and the ability to communicate directly through the platform enables clear expectations.

- Time Saving: By streamlining the process of finding, scheduling, and paying cleaners, you can focus more on other aspects of your business.

The success of your rental arbitrage business heavily depends on the cleanliness and management of your properties. Investing time and resources into finding reliable cleaning services, setting up an efficient property management system, and leveraging platforms like TurnoverBnB can significantly enhance your operational efficiency. These systems not only ensure a high-quality guest experience but also free up your time to focus on scaling and improving your business further. Remember, in the competitive world of short-term rentals, the cleanliness and smooth operation of your properties can make all the difference in achieving and maintaining a profitable portfolio.

Chapter 7

Rinse and Repeat

The journey to success in the Airbnb and VRBO rental arbitrage business doesn't end with setting up your first property. It's about continuously finding opportunities to expand, optimizing your operations, and planning for the future. This chapter will guide you through the process of growing your business, from acquiring additional properties to potentially buying your own and preparing your portfolio for sale.

Finding More Properties in the Area

Expanding your property portfolio in the same area can offer operational efficiencies and brand recognition among local travelers.

Strategies for Expansion

- Leverage Existing Relationships: Use the rapport you've built with current landlords to inquire about additional properties they might own or know about.

- Market Analysis: Continue using tools like AirDNA to identify high-demand areas where you can expand.

- Networking: Engage with local real estate agents and property managers who can alert you to potential rental opportunities.

Saving Money to Buy Your Own Property

While rental arbitrage is a fantastic way to enter the short-term rental market without owning property, eventually purchasing your own can offer more control and higher profit margins.

Financial Planning

- Reinvest Profits: Allocate a portion of your earnings towards a down payment fund.

- Explore Financing Options: Research loans and investment options to finance property purchases.

- Cost-Benefit Analysis: Consider the long-term benefits of owning versus leasing, including potential tax advantages and equity growth.

Scaling Your Business

Scaling involves not just adding more properties but also refining your operational processes to handle increased demand efficiently.

Tips for Scaling

- Automate and Delegate: Invest in technology and hire staff or virtual assistants to manage day-to-day operations.

- Maintain Quality: Ensure that the expansion doesn't compromise the quality of guest experiences.

- Diversify Your Portfolio: Look for different types of properties to appeal to a broader range of guests and mitigate risks associated with market fluctuations.

Preparing Your Portfolio to Be Sold

Whether you're looking to exit the business or pivot your strategy, preparing your portfolio for sale can maximize its value.

Steps for Preparation

- Financial Records: Keep detailed financial records, including income statements and occupancy rates, to demonstrate profitability to potential buyers.

- Operational Documentation: Create a comprehensive operations manual detailing your management processes, vendor contacts, and property maintenance schedules.

- Legal Compliance: Ensure all properties are compliant with local regulations and any lease agreements are transferable.

Ending Lease With Landlord

Should you decide to not renew a lease or need to end a lease early, handling the situation professionally is crucial.

Best Practices

- Notice and Communication: Provide ample notice as required by your lease agreement and communicate your intentions clearly and professionally.

- Property Condition: Return the property in the same or better condition than when you leased it, addressing any repairs or cleaning.

- Final Walk-Through: Schedule a final walk-through with the landlord to confirm the property's condition and settle any final matters.

Growing your Airbnb and VRBO rental arbitrage business requires a strategic approach to expansion, financial planning for future property acquisitions, and maintaining operational excellence. By continuously refining your business model, investing in properties, and preparing for potential exits, you can build a sustainable and profitable enterprise. The principles of "rinse and repeat" are not just about repetition but about learning, adapting, and thriving in the dynamic world of short-term rentals.

Chapter 8

Final Words

As we conclude our journey through the intricacies of building a successful Airbnb and VRBO Rental Arbitrage business, it's crucial to reflect on the path we've traversed, the lessons learned, and the future that lies ahead. This final chapter is dedicated to imparting some parting wisdom, highlighting the precautions and risks involved, and underscoring essential considerations to always keep in mind.

Embracing the Journey

Embarking on a rental arbitrage venture is more than starting a business; it's embracing a journey filled with learning, challenges, and opportunities for growth. Success in this field doesn't come overnight but through persistence, adaptability, and continuous improvement.

Precautions and Risks Involved

Regulatory Changes - The short-term rental landscape is continually evolving, with regulations and legal requirements that can change. Staying informed and compliant is paramount to avoid fines and legal issues that could jeopardize your business.

Market Fluctuations

Economic factors, tourism trends, and local events can all impact demand for short-term rentals. Diversifying your property portfolio and maintaining financial buffers can help mitigate these risks.

Property Damage

While rare, property damage by guests can occur. Implementing security deposits, vetting guests, and having comprehensive insurance are critical measures to protect your investment.

Things to Always Keep in Mind

Expanding your portfolio is important, but not at the expense of the quality of guest experiences. Each property should meet high standards to ensure guest satisfaction and positive reviews, which are the lifeblood of your business.

Continuous Learning

The short-term rental industry is dynamic, with new technologies, strategies, and best practices emerging regularly. Committing to ongoing education and staying abreast of industry trends will equip you to adapt and thrive.

Community Engagement

Engaging with the local community, whether through supporting local businesses or participating in community events, can enrich the experiences you offer guests and foster positive relationships with neighbors and local authorities.

Sustainability Practices

Incorporating eco-friendly practices and promoting sustainability can not only reduce operational costs but also appeal to a growing segment of environmentally conscious travelers.

Parting Thoughts

As you move forward with your Airbnb and VRBO rental arbitrage business, remember that each challenge is an opportunity for growth, and every guest experience is a chance to excel. The journey may not always be smooth, but the rewards—both financial and personal—can be significant.

Stay committed to providing exceptional experiences, be prepared to adapt to change, and always operate with integrity and professionalism.